FUNVERSATIONS

Witty Remarks and Fun Facts to Liven Up and "Laugh-en" Up Your Conversations

Stuart and Dave Clark

Bodley Creations

FUNVERSATIONS
Witty Remarks and Fun Facts to Liven Up and "Laugh-en" Up Your Conversations
Stuart and Dave Clark
Bodley Creations

Published by Bodley Creations, St. Louis, MO
Copyright ©2022 Bodley Creations
All rights reserved.

Cover and Interior design:
Davis Creative Publishing Partners, CreativePublishing Partners.com

Publisher's Cataloging-In-Publication Data

Names: Clark, Stuart, 1952- author. | Clark, Dave, 1954- author.
Title: Funversations : witty remarks and fun facts to liven up and "laugh-en" up your conversations / Stuart and Dave Clark.
Description: Revised and updated edition. | St. Louis, MO : Bodley Creations, 2022.
Identifiers: ISBN 9781737246220
Subjects: LCSH: American wit and humor. | Conversation. | LCGFT: Humor. | BISAC: HUMOR / Form / Jokes & Riddles. | GAMES & ACTIVITIES / General. | FAMILY & RELATIONSHIPS / General.
Classification: LCC PN6165 .C53 2022 | DDC 818.602--dc23

To Ann and Margaret

"Trouble knocked
at the door, but,
hearing laughter,
hurried away."
        -Benjamin Franklin

Table of Contents

INTRODUCTION

"Laughter is the shortest distance between two people"

Don't you just hate boring conversations? They're just so... boring! We don't want you ever to have to be stuck in one of those again. Be that guy or gal at the party that everyone wants to be around because you've mastered the art of turning conversations into funversations. The pages of this book are filled with witty remarks, fun facts and quirky one-liners for you to whip out at your next event and spice up your conversations.

For all of our adult lives, we have slipped most of these 187 lines or fun facts into casual conversations with our friends and family and have enjoyed the reactions that come with them. Some of them you've probably heard before somewhere, many of them will take you by surprise and we're hoping all of them make you smile.

This book is divided into 16 conversation topics from things like sports, marriage, diet and exercise, and aging. For the most part, we kept it very clean and the lines can be used in mixed company. But there are a few that we'd bump up to the not-so-scandalous rating of PG.

As savvy conversationalists are inclined to do, we steered clear of religion or politics. It's an old adage — religion and politics are the two things friends should probably not talk about in casual conversation. Those generally tend not to go over very well and we're in the business of creating smiles, not brawls.

Introduction

After reading through this book, you will no longer have to fake the need to go to the bathroom or get a beverage refill in order to dodge some awkward silence. You will no doubt collect some favorites to add to your arsenal and use them to infuse some laughter into any situation.

Now, let's turn those boring conversations into funversations!

Stuart and Dave

The Four Stages of Aging:

-First you forget names.
-Then you forget faces.
-Then you forget to pull your zipper up.
-Then you forget to pull your zipper down.

My grandmother lived
to be 98 and never
used glasses. She drank
straight from
the bottle.

In conversation, if you can't think of a word, say "I forgot the English word for it." That way people will think you're bilingual instead of an old idiot.

My memory's not as sharp as it used to be. Also, my memory's not as sharp as it used to be.

Like a lot of guys my age, I have a furniture problem. My chest has fallen into my drawers.

Yeah, I think I'm suffering from TMB:

Two Many Birthdays.

When I die,
I want to die like
my old grandfather
who died peacefully
in his sleep.
Not screaming like
all the passengers
in his car.

Growing old ain't
for sissies.

I was talking to two of my friends the other day about how it's the pits getting old and one friend said, "Every morning I get up at 6:30 to pee, but I have to stand at the toilet for three minutes waiting for my pee to come out."

"My other friend then said, "Every morning at 7:30 I have to poop, but I have to sit on the can for half an hour because of my constipation. It's terrible."

Then I said, "Well, the good news is for me, every morning at 6:30 I pee like a racehorse, then at 7:30 I poop like a pig. The bad news is, I don't wake up till 9 o'clock."

If I die in my bed, with my greedy in-laws gathered around me, I want my last words to be, "I left half a million dollars in cash under the, the…"

What does a pirate say on his 80th birthday? He says, "Aye, matey!" (I'm 80)

For bald/balding men
to say:

I had hair when I
needed it.

I was not happy when I found out that the staff at the nursing home was giving my grandfather Viagra at night right before he went to sleep. When I asked them why, they told me it was to keep him from rolling out of bed.

The best thing about being older is that I did all of my really stupid sh*t before cell phone cameras and YouTube.

Have you ever noticed that anyone on the road who is going faster than you is a maniac, and anyone going slower than you is a moron?

You can't turn
back the clock,
but you can always
wind it up again.

I asked my 98 year-old grandmother what was the best thing about being 98.
She said, "No peer pressure."

When you get old, everything hurts. When I get up in the morning it sounds like I'm making popcorn.

Getting older is
mandatory.
Getting old is optional.

WHEN YOU'RE WALKING WITH A LITTLE LIMP:

I've got a little hitch in my giddy-up.

One minute you're young and fun...
The next minute you're turning down the stereo in the car so you can see better.

I often read about people my age mountain climbing. Hey, I feel good getting my leg through my underwear without losing my balance.

I did a comedy gig at
an old folks home once.
They laughed so hard
at all my jokes.
I tell ya, there wasn't a
dry seat in the house.

I'm at a place in my life where errands are starting to count as going out.

As I've gotten older,
I find I interrupt people
more. I don't mean
to. I just randomly
remember things and
get really excited.

Age 80 might be
the new 60,
but 9:00 pm is
the new midnight.

ADVICE FOR DADS WITH YOUNG DAUGHTERS:

When you have a boy, you have one boy to worry about. When you have a *girl*, you have *every boy* in the world to worry about.

When my kids are giving me a headache, I follow the directions on the aspirin bottle, especially the part that says, "Keep away from children."

To your kids who want
to do something that
you don't want them
to:

The short answer is
"No!"
The long answer is
"Hell, no!"

When your kids are little, you can eat them with a spoon. When they're teenagers, you wish you had.

A COMMENT GRANDPARENTS CAN MAKE ABOUT THEIR CHILDREN AND GRANDCHILDREN COMING TO VISIT THEM:

"We love to see the headlights, but it's also nice to see the tail lights."

Never doubt the courage of the French. They were the ones who discovered that snails are edible.

My mom's cooking...
I gotta say this about
it...it filled you up...
IF you could keep it
down.

My wife's cooking is so bad that we pray after we eat.

With my wife's cooking
we know dinner is
ready when the smoke
alarm goes off.

The best thing my wife
makes for dinner is
reservations.

I was ready to leave the restaurant and I had some food still on my plate. Pointing to my leftover food the waiter asked me, "Do you wanna box for that?" I said, "No, but I'll wrestle you for it."

Acceptable work
That's close enough for government work.

Boastful person
He can strut sitting down.

Brave person
Brave as the first man who ate an oyster.

Busy person

He's so busy you'd think he was twins.

Capable, experienced person

Don't worry about the mule. Just load the wagon.

No problem. I'm on that like stink on a monkey.

Cheap person
He's tight as wallpaper.

He has short arms and low pockets.

When he takes a dollar bill out of his wallet, George Washington blinks from the light.

Crazy person
The porch light's on but nobody's home.

Hot weather

It's so hot outside the trees are bribing the dogs.

Inept, worthless person

He couldn't hit water if he fell out of a boat.

Not impressed by person's bragging
Big deal. Whaddaya want me to do? Send up a bottle rocket?

Give me the bacon without the sizzle.

Short person
She's so short that when she farts dust flies.

Sick person

I feel like I've been eaten by a wolf and sh*t off a cliff.

Stupid person

I can explain it to you, but I can't understand it for you.

The difference between genius and stupidity is that genius has its limits.

I'm a Tough guy
I'll knock you into the middle of next week.

There are 10 mean S.O.B.s in this world and 9 of them send me Christmas cards.

Unwanted friend
Hey, anytime you happen to pass my house, I'd sure appreciate it.

You have to stay in shape. My grandmother, she started walking five miles a day when she was 60. She's 97 today and we have no idea where she is.

Have you heard about the new U.S. Ski Team diet? I just started on it and it's working great. What you do is you put on a pair of snow skis inside your house. That way, when you walk into the kitchen, (stretch out your arm in front of you) you can't reach the cabinets where the cookies are or open the freezer for ice cream...

Yesterday morning I needed to be really alert for a meeting I was having at my office. So instead of using water for making my coffee in the kitchen, I used that high energy drink, Red Bull. I hurried off to my meeting. Man, I was halfway to work before I realized I had forgotten my car.

If you had to decide between sticking to your diet and eating a piece of chocolate, would you prefer dark or milk chocolate?

I decided to stop calling the bathroom the "John" and renamed it after another man's name: the "Jim."
I feel so much better saying I went to the Jim this morning.

If we shouldn't eat late night snacks, why do they put a light in the fridge?

Believe me, I would go to the gym more often if it had a smoking section.

When I look at chocolate, I hear two voices in my head.

The first one says: "You need to eat that chocolate."

The other voice goes: "You heard correctly. Now eat the chocolate."

There are only three
things that don't lie.
Small children.
Drunk people.
And yoga pants.

My wife wanted to lose some weight so she placed a picture of a real shapely, pinup model on our refrigerator to remind her of her goal.
The reminder worked like a charm for her. She lost ten pounds in the first month of using this method.
The bad news was that I ended up gaining fifteen pounds.

I'm on that new garlic and onion diet.

You don't actually lose weight, but you look thinner from a distance.

I'm in shape.
Round is a shape.

The Internet went down at our house, so I had to spend time with the family. They seem like good people.

When you're the father
of the bride, there are
only three rules you
need to follow:
Show up, Shut up
and Pay up.

Every family's got a crazy uncle. In most parts of the country, they hide him in the basement. In the South, they/we put him on the front porch and give him a cocktail.

If evolution really works, how come mothers only have two hands?

What did our parents do to kill boredom before the Internet? I asked my 18 brothers and sisters and they didn't know either.

How many of us have looked around at our family reunion and thought "Well, aren't we just two clowns short of a circus?"

When I was a kid and there were no seatbelts in cars, I would ride in the front seat with my grandmother. She would throw her right arm out in front of me when she had to quickly stop the car. The flabby fat hanging under her arm served as a really good airbag.

I grew up with four brothers and sisters. That's how I learned to dance...waiting to use the one bathroom in our house.

Did you know that 2 to 3 glasses of wine a day can reduce your risk of giving a sh*t?

The best medicine to stop a cough is a large dose of laxatives. Then you don't dare cough.

My doctor has advised me to stop drinking. It's going to be a really big change for me. I've been with that doctor for 15 years.

The worst time to have a heart attack is during a game of charades.

Die young as late as
possible.

When tempted to fight fire with fire, remember that the Fire Department usually uses water.

I hate it when people use big words just to make themselves sound perspicacious*.

*Adjective: Insightful, acutely intelligent and wise

If you can't fix it with a hammer, you've got an electrical problem.

Accept the fact that some days you're the pigeon and some days you're the statue.

Never slap a man who's chewing tobacco.

A wise man once said,

"Remember to
always be yourself.
Unless you really suck."

Never kick a fresh turd
on a hot day.

The early bird may get the worm, but it's the second mouse that gets the cheese.

24 hours in day.
24 beers in a case.
Coincidence?
I think not.

A good friend once told me that if your life is consumed by wine, women and song... you need to give up singing.

If you don't read the newspapers, you're uninformed. If you do read the newspapers, you're misinformed.

If I ever go missing,
I want my picture on
a wine bottle not
a milk carton.
I want FUN people
to find me.

The true nature of a human being clearly shows up when the supermarket announces that a second cash register is now open.

When I hear somebody sigh, "Life is hard," I am always tempted to ask, "Compared to what?"

We do not stop playing
because we grow old;
we grow old because
we stop playing.

Some people cause
happiness wherever
they go.
Others whenever
they go.

Put a mouse trap on top of your alarm clock. It will prevent you from rolling over and going back to sleep after you hit the snooze button.

You only need two
tools for doing
projects:
WD-40 and duct tape.
If it doesn't move and
should, use WD-40.
If it shouldn't move
and does, use the
duct tape.

I didn't say it was your fault. I just said I was blaming you.

I changed my password to "incorrect" so that whenever I forget it, the computer will say, "Your password is incorrect."

Trust everyone,
but cut the cards.

Lord, give me patience. Because if you give me strength, I'll need bail money to go with it.

When the Conversation is on Love and Marriage

This happened back when my wife and I first started dating. Keep in mind that she had gone to an all-girls high school so she was pretty naive when it came to dating guys.

One night, she and I were in the front seat of my car kissing. Well, we got to making out really good there in my front seat so I stopped and whispered to her, "Do you want to get in the back seat?" She said "No."

Continued on next page

So we continued to make out some more and in a little while, again I asked her, "Do you want to get in the back seat?" Again she told me, "No."

Well, we kept making out and after a couple more minutes I asked her one more time, "Do you want to get in the back seat?" And again she said, "No."

Finally, I said, "Why not?" She said "I want to be in the front seat with you."

My wife's credit card got stolen. I didn't report it because the thief charges less on it that my wife did.

There's a new study about married women and how they feel about their asses. The results were very interesting. 10% of women think their ass is too skinny. 40% of women think their ass is too fat.

And 50% say they don't care WHAT their husband looks like.

You don't marry the person who you can live with.
You marry the person who you cannot live without.

If a man said he'll fix it, he'll fix it. There is no need to nag him every 6 months about it.

Honey, when you
ask me what I am
doing today, and I say
"nothing," it does not
mean I am free.
It means I am doing
nothing.

My wife is so fertile, she can get pregnant just folding my underwear.

My wife and I went to a marriage counselor and the marriage counselor says to me, "Your wife says you never buy her flowers. Is that true?" I said "To be honest, I never knew she sold flowers."

My wife didn't order anything from Amazon in the last couple of days so the delivery guy knocked on the door to see if we were okay.

I was struggling to get my wife's attention. So I simply sat down and looked comfortable. That did the trick.

If momma ain't happy,
nobody's happy.

The secret to our
35 years of marriage?
My wife and I have this
understanding that
goes way back to when
we first got married...
I don't try to run HER
life. And I don't try to
run MY life.

Right after my husband/wife and I got married, we decided that for the rest of our marriage, we'd go out twice a week. Nice candlelight dinner. Soft music. A little dancing. It's worked great.
He/She goes out on Tuesdays.
I go out on Fridays.

When I married
Mr. Right, I had no
idea his first name
was "Always."

When we first got married, we made a pact. In our life together, it was decided I would make all of the big decisions and my wife would make all of the little decisions. For X years now, we have held true to that agreement. Funny thing is that in our X years of marriage, there hasn't been one big decision.

We've been married for almost ___ years. Seems like five minutes... under water.

If I agreed with you, dear, then we'd both be wrong.

Observation on why husbands and wives are not as loving and attentive to each other as they were when they were dating:

"When you catch the bus, you stop running."

Right after my wife and I got married, I sat her down and told her that I was the boss of the house and that she would be doing all the housework and cooking and that she could spend only the allowance I gave her. She got really mad and was so upset that I didn't see her for three days.

...On the third day I could barely see her out of the corner of this eye (pretend to pry open a corner of that one eye).

Sometimes I wake up grumpy; other times I let her/him sleep.

My father once told me, "Son, it's time you got married. Happiness isn't the only thing in life."

You know the Andy Griffith Show. The reason Mayberry was so peaceful and quiet was because nobody was married. Andy, Barney, Aunt Bea, Gomer, Goober, Floyd, Howard, Earnest T. Bass, Helen, Thelma Lou, Clara. The only married person was Otis, and he stayed drunk.

Give a man a fish and he will eat for a day. Teach him how to fish and he will sit in a boat and drink beer all day.

If you gave (name of a known big blowhard) an enema, you could carry him around in a match box.

When a friend jokingly calls you a derogatory name like "butt head," say back to him, "Hey pal, that's MISTER butt head to you!"

That guy is always so wound up. He makes coffee nervous.

There is a very easy way to come back from a casino with a small fortune.
Go there with a large one.

You know what I'd do when I win the lottery? I'll spend 90% on good times, women, and whiskey.
The other 10%, I'll probably waste.

The recession has hit me really hard. Would you believe I got a pre-declined credit card in the mail?

My stockbroker/The stock market made me a millionaire... I used to be a multi-millionaire.

If you lend someone $20 and you never see or hear from that person again... it's probably the best $20 you ever spent.

Rock & Roll Hall of Fame Snubs

Being that the likes of the 10 rock and roll groups listed on the next page from the 1960's and 70's era have all been inducted into the Rock and Roll Hall of Fame, there should be NO good reason that the list of 20 rock performers shown after them shouldn't also be inducted into the Hall.

PERSPECTIVE:
10 Current Hall of Fame members

The Animals
The Dave Clark Five
The Loving Spoonful
Buffalo Springfield
The Byrds
The Yardbirds
The Hollies
The Ventures
The O'Jays
The Shirelles

20 deserving ones that have been snubbed (as of 3/1/2021)
(In alphabetical order)

The Association

Their ballads "Cherish" and "Never My Love" are among the most played songs in history. And "Windy" and "Along Comes Mary" are other classics.

The Carpenters

Some may say they're too lightweight to be considered rock but Karen Carpenter's voice is a thing of beauty, and they made wonderful pop records.

Chubby Checker

He took "The Twist" to #1 twice, in two different years. Give the man his due already!

Cher

Is she rock? Probably more so than Madonna, who's been inducted. And let's not forget those good times with Sonny.

Jim Croce

His life was cut short before he had a chance to truly develop but the trove of hits he left behind was substantial.

The Crystals

Even more than the Ronettes, the Crystals were Phil Spector's go-to girl group. Darlene Love and La La Brooks were (and still are) dynamic singers. Their 1961–1964 chart hits, including "There's No Other (Like My Baby)," "Uptown," "He's Sure the Boy I Love," "He's a Rebel," "Da Doo Ron Ron" and "Then He Kissed Me."

Foreigner

Few mainstream arena-rock bands were bigger in the late '70s/'80s, and anthems like "Hot Blooded" and "Cold as Ice" are emblematic of that era's radio-friendly mindset.

Lesley Gore

"It's My Party," "Judy's Turn to Cry," "Sunshine, Lollipops, and Rainbows," "You Don't Own Me" and so many more hits. She was every teenage girl's BFF in the 60's.

The Grass Roots

Easy to forget them until you look at their long string of smashes: "Midnight Confessions," "Let's Live for Today," "Temptation Eyes" "Sooner or Later" and many more.

The Guess Who

The Canadian band led by Burton Cummings and Randy Bachman was another hit machine: "American Woman," "These Eyes," "No Sugar Tonight."

Herman's Hermits

They weren't hugely popular only because singer Peter Noone was "cute." They also made many, many durable pop hits. Such as: "I'm into Something Good," "Silhouettes," "Can't You Hear My Heartbeat," "Wonderful World," "Leaning on the Lamp Post," "I'm Henry the Eighth, I Am," "There's a Kind of Hush All Over the World" and "Mrs. Brown, You've Got a Lovely Daughter."

Tommy James and the Shondells

"Crimson and Clover," "Mony, Mony," "Crystal Blue Persuasion" and, of course, "Hanky Panky." So many hits, all very diverse.

Jay and the Americans

The Rock & Roll Hall of Fame has acknowledged many great vocal groups, but one of the best — Jay & the Americans — has yet to be cited despite numerous big hits throughout the 1960's. Such As: "Come A Little Bit Closer," "Cara, Mia," "She Cried," "This Magic Moment," "Some Enchanted Evening," "Walkin' In The Rain," "Let's Lock the Door."

The Monkees

Enough with the "didn't play their own instruments" excuse. (Neither did The Supremes, The Temptations, The Righteous Brothers, etc.). Their numerous big hit records were some of the finest pop-rock of the era, and their influence on the rock video medium was incalculable.

Paul Revere and the Raiders

With charismatic frontman Mark Lindsay, they released hit after hit: "Kicks," "Hungry," "Just Like Me," and "Good Thing."

Johnny Rivers

No one reimagined others' songs as deliciously: "Poor Side of Town," "Mountain of Love," "Memphis," "Secret Agent Man," "Baby I Need Your Lovin'," "Summer Rain." He was a constant presence on the charts for years.

Diana Ross

As if she hadn't already broken enough ground with The Supremes, Ross then went on to have a huge solo career, with #1 hits like "Upside Down" and "Touch Me in the Morning."

Three Dog Night

If we judge Hall of Fame nominees by the impact they had in their own time, then Three Dog Night deserves a look. Hit after hit after hit.

The Turtles

The L.A. band was one of the few that didn't use studio musicians, and they came up with "Happy Together," "She'd Rather Be With Me," "Elenore," "You Baby" and more. That's impressive.

SPORTS FUN FACT #1

There's one sport in which neither the spectators nor the participants know the score or who's winning until the contest ends.

Answer: Boxing

SPORTS FUN FACT #2

What are the only two days of the year on which no professional sports games are played in the United States?

ANSWER: The only two days of the entire year on which no professional sports games are played in the United States are the day before and the day after the All-Star Game for Major League Baseball.

SPORTS FUN FACT #3

Only three sports movies have won Best Picture in Oscar history. How many can you name?
Hints: Two of the three had a boxing plot; the other was track and field.
One of the three was based on a true story.

ANSWER:
Rocky (1976-boxing), Chariots of Fire (1981-track and field film and true story during the 1924 Olympics), and Million Dollar Baby (2004-boxing).

SPORTS FUN FACT #4

ATHLETES WHO WON THE MOST MVP AWARDS IN THEIR SPORT

NFL: PEYTON MANNING, 5

MLB: BARRY BONDS, 7
There are many out there who want to put asterisks next to all of Bonds' achievements, but three of those MVP awards happened before he was widely believed to have begun juicing — and no other player in baseball history has won the MVP more than three times.

NBA: KAREEM ABDUL-JABBAR, 6

NHL: WAYNE GRETZKY, 9
Gretzky won the MVP Hart Trophy 8 consecutive years from 1980-87.

SPORTS FUN FACT #5

While there has never been
a three-peat (3 consecutive
championships) with an NFL
Super Bowl champ, the NBA
(8 in a row 1959-66-Boston
Celtics), NHL (5 in a row
1956-60-Montreal Canadians)
and MLB (5 in a row 1949-
53-NY Yankees) have each
featured multiple such
championships.

BASEBALL

Did you know that baseball is mentioned in the Bible? As a matter of fact, it's in the very first line:

"In the beginning (in the big inning)"

BASEBALL

BASEBALL FUN FACT #1
Besides getting a base hit single, there are seven ways a baseball player can officially reach first base. Name them.

(Next page)

1. Error (at-bat charged to hitter)
2. Hit by pitch (no at-bat charged to hitter)
3. Fielder's Choice (at-bat charged to hitter)
4. Base on balls (no at-bat charged to hitter)
5. Dropped third strike by the catcher (at-bat charged to hitter)
6. Catcher's interference with the batter (no at-bat charged to hitter)
7. Defensive obstruction with the batter/runner (no at-bat charged to hitter)

BASEBALL

BASEBALL FUN FACT #2

What baseball pitcher holds the record for losing the most games in major league history?

HINT: An award named after this pitcher is given annually to the best pitchers in Major League Baseball.

ANSWER: Denton "Cy" Young. He lost 316 games, but he also won more games (511) than any other major league pitcher in history-thus the Cy Young award.

BASEBALL

BASEBALL FUN FACT #3
There are 18 minutes of total
action in a baseball game.
Source: study reported in the
Wall Street Journal

BASEBALL

BASEBALL FUN FACT #4

On July 2, 1963, San Francisco Giants' Juan Marichal vs. Milwaukee Braves' Warren Spahn at Candlestick Park remains among baseball's greatest pitching duels — two future Hall of Famers going toe-to-toe for 4 hours and 10 minutes. On that day Marichal pitched a 16-inning shutout outdueling Spahn. Willie Mays won the game 1-0 with a home run.

Marichal threw 227 pitches;
Spahn threw 201.
(In today's ML game a
starting pitcher will usually
be removed from the game
after 100 pitches, regardless of
the actual number of innings
pitched).
Spahn was 42 years old and
in the last of his 13 20-win
seasons; Marichal was 25 and
on his way to winning 20
games for the first time.

BASEBALL

BASEBALL FUN FACT #5

In 2004, home run king Barry Bonds was intentionally walked 120 times. How many times was Roger Maris intentionally walked the year he hit 61 home runs?

Answer: ZERO. Mickey Mantle batted behind him.

NBA BASKETBALL

NBA BASKETBALL FUN FACT

Wilt Chamberlain didn't win the MVP award the year he scored 50.4 points and grabbed 25.7 rebounds per game (1962). The Boston Celtic's Bill Russell won it that year, getting 51 first place votes to Chamberlain's 9.

NFL FOOTBALL

NFL FUN FACT #1

The first Super Bowl took place on January 15, 1967 (NFL's Green Bay Packers vs. the AFL's Kansas City Chiefs) The game tickets were only $12.00.

The first game is the only Super Bowl in history that didn't sell out. The Los Angeles Coliseum is huge, and attendance for the game was only 61,946 out of 100,594 seats.

NFL FOOTBALL

NFL FUN FACT #2
In 2021, the cost of a
30-second commercial during
Super Bowl LV set a new
record — $5.6 million.

NFL FOOTBALL

NFL FUN FACT #3

An average NFL football game lasts 3 hours and 12 minutes, but if you tally up the time when the ball is actually in play, the action amounts to a mere 11 minutes. An average play in the NFL last just four seconds.

Of course, watching football on TV is hardly just about the game; there are plenty of advertisements too. The average NFL game includes 20 commercial breaks containing more than 100 ads

Source: study reported in the *Wall Street Journal*

MEN'S COLLEGE BASKETBALL

MEN'S COLLEGE BASKETBALL FUN FACT

When the UCLA Bruins lost a basketball game on January 19th, 1974, it ended a streak of 88 consecutive victories, which coincidentally began exactly three years earlier on January 19, 1971.

The streak of 88 consecutive wins is still an active Division I men's basketball streak.

GOLF

I play in the low 80's.
If it gets any warmer than that, I
don't play.

GOLF

I've written three articles for
Golf Digest:

"How to Get More Distance Out
of Your Shanks,"

"Ricochet, My Way," and

"Proper Stances to Take on
Your Fourth Putt."

GOLF

To give you an idea of how bad my golf game is, I just had my ball retriever re-gripped.

GOLF

You can talk to a fade, but a hook won't listen.

GOLF

Playing golf today, I only hit two good balls. It's when I stepped on a rake in the sand trap.

GOLF

One day I'm going to shoot my age. But right now, I'm having trouble shooting my weight.

BOWLING

I knew a guy who bowled a 301 (300 and WON).

People who know the game of bowling will say that bowling a game over 300 is impossible. You then say:

Did you ever hear about a guy bowling a 300 and LOSE?

SWIMMING

I got caught peeing in our club's swimming pool yesterday. The lifeguard must have seen me. He blew his whistle so loud I almost fell in.

Yeah, I left two (name a local really bad college or pro sports team) tickets on the dashboard of my car. When I got back I found my window broken...and 12 more tickets.

You show me a good loser and I'll show you a loser.

UNITED STATES FUN FACT #1

How many states are there in the United States?
ANSWER: Most people, of course, will say that there are 50 states. But, technically there are only 46 "states." The other four are officially designated as "commonwealths": Virginia, Massachusetts, Pennsylvania, and Kentucky. Every legal document concerning these four places read "commonwealth of Virginia, etc.," not "state of." This designation has no constitutional impact. The word commonwealth is of English derivation and refers to the common "wealth" or welfare of the public. In common parlance, people do not make the distinction between state and commonwealth.

UNITED STATES FUN FACT #2

Is it possible for people living in a state that borders the Pacific Ocean and people living in a state that borders the Atlantic Ocean to ever share the exact same time?

ANSWER: YES, thanks to daylight saving time and time zones, parts of states on the Pacific and the Atlantic coasts do share the same time for one hour each year.

When we transition from daylight savings time to standard time in the fall, adjacent time zones share time for an hour. For example, the Central Time zone "falls back" to standard time and matches the Mountain Time still in daylight savings time until it falls back an hour later.

The very eastern part of Oregon (a Pacific coast state) is in Mountain Time and the western panhandle of Florida (an Atlantic coast state) is in Central Time. Because the Mountain and Central Time's zones are adjacent, parts of Oregon and Florida will have the exact same time for one hour when the Central Time Zone "falls back" each year.

This could end in 2023 if the daylight savings time bill passes.

UNITED STATES FUN FACT #3

Three of the first five U.S. presidents died on Independence Day, July 4th. Can you name them?
ANSWER: John Adams and Thomas Jefferson both died on July 4th, 1826, the 50th anniversary of the country's birth. James Monroe, the fifth president, died on July 4th, five years later in 1831.

UNITED STATES FUN FACT #4

John Tyler, the 10th President of the United States; the sixth president before Abraham Lincoln, was born in 1790...231 years ago. One of his grandsons is still alive. True or false?

ANSWER: TRUE. It seems very remarkable, but one grandson of John Tyler (the 10th president of the United States and a man born in 1790, less than a year after George Washington was first inaugurated as president) is still alive (as of April 2022).

HOW IS THIS POSSIBLE?
The Tyler men have a habit of having kids very late in life. Lyon Gardiner Tyler, one of President Tyler's 15 kids, was born in 1853. He fathered Harrison Ruffin Tyler in 1928.

Check it out on Snopes or Google.

FACT: the average man owns 12 pairs of shoes, while the average women owns 27 pairs of shoes. A recent survey found that 85% of women have purchased a pair of shoes that are still sitting in their closets and have never been worn.

There are two excellent theories for arguing with women. Unfortunately, neither one works.

Don't wait until you know a girl better before you kiss her. Kiss her and you'll know her better.

A woman's love is like the morning dew.
It's just as likely to fall on a rose petal as it is on a horse turd.

Men, try this in front of your guy friends:

"Man, I saw this beautiful chick today who was like this!"

Then cup both of your hands and hold them about 8-10 inches in front of your chest depicting large breasts. Make sure to bend your fingers in slightly. Then, while still holding out your cupped hands, surprise them by saying with a concerned face,

"Yeah, she had arthritis in both hands.
...Well, what were you guys thinking?"

Women dress for women. If women dressed for men, the stores wouldn't sell much. Just an occasional sun visor.

TRAVEL

I hate those Ritz Carlton
bath towels.
They're too big.
I can't fit them in my
suitcase.

HEARING AIDS

You'll need a partner on this one. Say to him/her that you're about to tell everyone in the group of friends you're with how great your new very expensive hearing aid is (even if you don't wear one). Tell your chosen sidekick partner to ask you when you pause from bragging about your new hearing aid, "Hey, what KIND is it?"
You look at your watch and say "Umm, it's two o'clock (or whatever time it really is)".

ANCIENT ROME

Make the letter V with two fingers, show the V to your friends, holding your hand up high, and ask them, "What is this?" They'll probably say it's a peace sign or a victory sign.
Say "No, it's Julius Caesar ordering five beers at the gladiator fights."
(V is the Roman numeral for 5)

DONATING BLOOD

I tried donating blood today...NEVER AGAIN!!! (Pause. Wait for the question "Why? What happened?" Then say...) They ask too many stupid questions: "Whose blood is this?" "Where did you get it from?" "Why is it in a bucket?"

WANT TO MAKE A TON OF MONEY FOR THE REST OF YOUR LIFE?

Write ONE hit Christmas song.

The #2 all-time money making Christmas song: Mariah Carey & Walter Afanasieff "All I Want For Christmas Is You" (1994). The song, which reportedly only took 15 minutes to write, generates an estimated $600,000 per year in royalties for Walter and Mariah, $60 million to date.

Continued on next page

AND #1 all-time money making Christmas song: Irving Berlin – "White Christmas" (1940).
The Guinness Book of World Records has named "White Christmas" the best selling single of all time.
$65 million earned to date.

CATS

The other day I accidentally ran over a cat that belonged to my old lady neighbor. I went up to her house and apologized to her. But then I opened my big mouth and told her that I'd like to REPLACE her cat. Well, she gladly took me up on my offer ...So damn, every day for an hour now I have to go sit on her lap and purr.

TOILET PAPER

They ought to name that toilet tissue "John Wayne" toilet paper. It's rough and tough and doesn't take sh!t off anybody.

SMALL TOWNS

I came from a small country town. Its population always stayed exactly the same. As soon as a baby was born a man left town.

COUNTRY MUSIC

Here are some humorous Country Song titles you can inject into the conversation on music.

1.) If The Phone Don't Ring, You Know It's Me

2.) Get Your Tongue Out Of My Mouth, I'm Tryin' To Kiss You Goodbye

3.) I'd Rather Have A Bottle In Front Of Me Than A Frontal Lobotomy

4.) It's Hard To Kiss The Lips At Night That Chewed My Ass Out All Day Long

5.) I'm So Miserable Without You, It's Almost Like Having You Here

6.) If I Can't Be Your Number One, Then Number Two On You

7.) My Wife Ran Away With My Best Friend and I Miss Him

8.) I Kissed Her On The Lips, And Left Her Behind For You

9.) I Still Miss You...But My Aim's Gettin' Better

10.) How Can I Miss You If You Won't Go Away?

11.) Thank God and Greyhound She's Gone

12.) If I Had Shot You When I Wanted To, I'd Be Out By Now

THE WEATHER

It's so hot....I left the toilet seat up today just to get an icy stare from my wife.

AUTO REPAIR

My ace auto mechanic told me that he couldn't fix my brakes, so he just decided to make my horn louder.

GOOD OLD DAYS

Things are so different these days. I remember when I was a kid I could go to the candy store with just a dollar in my pocket.
I could get two candy bars, a pack of Hostess cupcakes and a bottle of soda pop.
...Nowadays they have cameras everywhere.

**WHEN YOU DON'T
FEEL LIKE GIVING A STANDARD
REPLY TO "HOW YA DOING?"**

Life is great! I've got a wife and
a color TV and they both work.

THE GERMAN LANGUAGE

I only know one word in German. It's the word for brassiere.
Stoppemfrumfloppin.

HERE'S A PHRASE YOU MAY WANT TO MEMORIZE AND USE ON OCCASION:

"The nonjudgmental ongoing reassessment of ego differentiation facilitates role adjustment in the interrelation of consensus work combining self-determination with an authoritative structured environment."

The sentence above is merely a grouping of long words. It means absolutely nothing. But it sure sounds real intelligent. Take time to memorize it and use it, as a joke, to sound intellectual (for just a minute) to friends in given situations.

Continued on next page

For example, you may use the sentence if a friend asks you "what's new?" Instead of just saying the old regular "Not much." or "Same ol' same ol'" you might say, "Well, I've been preparing for a speech I have to give to a large group of people next week. It's about a hotly debated subject: 'The nonjudgmental ongoing reassessment...blah, blah, blah... structured environment'".

Say this with a serious look and don't smile when you finish. Wait for your friend's response. Then you can laugh.

You can come up with lots of fun ways to slip this sentence into your conversations.

CELEBRITY GOSSIP

You: "Did you hear about the famous actress who stabbed her husband for cheating? Reese...something. Reese... Reese..."

Friend: "Witherspoon?"

You: "No, with a knife."

BAD DRIVING

My daughter got 8 out of 10 on her driver's test. The other two guys managed to jump out of her way.

BAD DRIVING

When you're riding in a car that the driver is making turns way too fast on city streets, ask him,

"Are there any penguins in (name the city you are driving in)?"

After he says "no," say,

"Well, then, sh*t, I think you just ran over two nuns."

BAD SINGING

Your friend is singing some familiar song. You ask him,

"Hey, who sang that song?"

Wait for his answer (i.e. "the Beatles")... you say,

"Uhh, let's keep it that way."

TOO MUCH TO DRINK

What I don't like about office Christmas parties is always having to look for a new job the next day.

TOO MUCH TO DRINK

I went out drinking last night so I took the bus home.

That might not be a big deal to you but I've never driven a bus before.

TOO MUCH TO DRINK

When someone asks what you did over the weekend, squint and ask, "Why, what did you hear?"

MILITARY SERVICE

When asked if you served in the military, say,

"No, but I did my part. During the _____War, I felt I needed to stay home to boost up the morale of the women."

MILITARY SERVICE

My great-great-grandfather was a famous Civil War general. He once had a Red Cross nurse shot from underneath him during battle.

COVID 19

I've been really scrubbing my hands so much this year. Suddenly, today I saw some faint writing on my hand. I looked closely and finally figured that, wow, it was the answers to my 8th grade Social Studies test.

THANKSGIVING

Ask a friend when it gets close to Thanksgiving time:

"How do you keep a turkey in suspense?"

Just keep quiet and look right into the eyes of the "turkey" who is waiting in suspense for your answer.
Then smile after he gets it.

ABOUT THE AUTHORS

Growing up in a small town, Kirkwood, Missouri, Stuart and Dave Clark enjoyed an exciting childhood, sparking an artistic collaboration that has lasted a lifetime. They've had numerous creative ventures, including a successful line of humorous greeting cards sold through Recycled Paper Greetings called "Quote/UnQuote." Stu and Dave have also created two board games. "Out of Character" was their first game venture, and "Letter Rip" produced by University Games, is their latest. They have one previous book called *Living Up to Your Eulogy*.